This book belongs to

_____

Helen Keller

By Mary Nhin

Illustrated By
Yuliia Zolotova

This book is dedicated to my children - Mikey, Kobe, and Jojo.

Copyright © 2022 by Grow Grit Press LLC. All rights reserved. No part of this book may be reproduced in any form without permission in writing from the publisher. Please send bulk order requests to growgritpress@gmail.com
978-1-63731-404-3 Printed and bound in the USA. MiniMovers.tv

When I was a baby, I became very sick with an illness. Eventually, I got better, but I lost both my hearing and my vision after the illness.

I used sign language to communicate, but many people couldn't understand me.

Imagine not being able to talk or see.
I felt sad and lonely.

My parents found a special instructor to help me. My teacher was very kind and her name was Anne Sullivan. Anne taught me how to communicate by using new methods. She did this by spelling words letter by letter with her fingers into the palm of my hand.

This was really amazing to me. I had no idea that there were so many different wonderful things in the world with their own unique names!

When it came time, I was very excited to go to a special school for the deaf. I worked hard to learn how to read and write.

When I got older, I applied and was accepted into Harvard University.

I communicated by using braille and sign language using my hands.

More importantly, I learned to speak using my voice.

I never let my disabilities stop me. I became a highly requested public speaker, traveling around the world.

And I used my voice to advocate for the rights of people with disabilities.

I dedicated myself to showing people what could be accomplished with opportunity and hard work. I wanted others with disabilities to know that they too can accomplish whatever their heart desires.

Life is either a daring adventure or nothing.

Timeline

1903 – Helen publishes her first book, an autobiography

1919 – Helen appears in a film telling the story of her life

1964 – Helen is awarded the Presidential Medal of Freedom

1973 – Helen is inducted into the National Women's Hall of Fame

minimovers.tv

@marynhin   @GrowGrit
#minimoversandshakers

Mary Nhin   Ninja Life Hacks

Ninja Life Hacks

@ninjalifehacks.tv

www.ingramcontent.com/pod-product-compliance
Lightning Source LLC
Chambersburg PA
CBHW041522070526
44585CB00002B/52